CRANES

Ann Becker

This edition first published in 2010 in the United States of America by Marshall Cavendish Benchmark.

Marshall Cavendish Benchmark
99 White Plains Road
Tarrytown, NY 10591
www.marshallcavendish.us

Library of Congress Cataloging-in-Publication Data

Becker, Ann, 1965-
   Cranes / by Ann Becker.
        p. cm. -- (Amazing machines)
        Summary: "Discusses the different kinds of cranes, what they are used for, and how they work"--Provided by publisher.
        Includes bibliographical references and index.
        ISBN 978-0-7614-4401-5
1. Cranes--Juvenile literature. I. Title.
        TJ1363.B343 2010
        621.8'73--dc22
        2008054368

The photographs in this book are used by permission and through the courtesy of:
t=top b=bottom c=center l=left r=right m=middle
Cover Photos: Millraw|/iStockphoto; Andy/iStockphoto; (Inset): Jean Christopher/Fotolia, Background: kertlis/iStockphoto;
Title Photo: Zygimantas Cepaitis/Fotolia
Content Page: Background: kertlis/iStockphoto

4-5: Alex Nikada/iStockphoto; 6-7: Zygimantas Cepaitis/Fotolia; 7(inset): Kamil Sobócki/Shutterstock; 8-9: Dan70/Shutterstock; 9(inset): jan kranendonk/Shutterstock; 10: Diane N. Ennis/Shutterstock; 11(inset): Kamil Sobócki/Shutterstock; 12-13: Eremin Sergey/Shutterstock; 13(inset): Richmatts/iStockphoto; 14: JoLin/Shutterstock; 15(inset): AVTG/iStockphoto; 16-17: Justin Kase zonez / Alamy; 17(inset): Al Messerschmidt/Contributor/Getty Images; 18-19: Eric Middelkoop/Shutterstock; 19(inset): Miguel Angel Pallardo del Rio/Shutterstock; 20-21: Pixonnet.com / Alamy; 21(inset): Tammy616/iStockphoto; 22: JoLin/Shutterstock; 23(inset): Stephen Coburn/Shutterstock; 24-25: Transtock/Corbis; 25(inset): Merrill Dyck/Shutterstock; 26L: Kamil Sobócki/Shutterstock; 26R:Tammy616/iStockphoto; 27L: AVTG/iStockphoto; 27R: jan kranendonk/Shutterstock; 28-29BG: kertlis/iStockphoto; 29: Valery Potapova/Shutterstock; 30-31: Anyka/Shutterstock; 32: kertlis/iStockphoto.

Art Director: Sumit Charles

Client Service Manager: Santosh Vasudevan

Project Manager: Shekhar Kapur

Editor: Penny Dowdy

Designer: Ritu Chopra

Photo Researcher: Shreya Sharma

Printed in Malaysia
1 3 5 6 4 2

Contents

What Is a Crane?

A **crane** is a machine that raises, lowers, and moves things. Cranes can be part of trucks and trains. They can also be part of a building, like a factory.

Cranes are very helpful in lifting heavy objects. People use cranes when normal tools cannot lift the weight.

Cranes help people raise heavy objects to high places.

5

Mobile Crane

A **mobile crane** runs on wheels. *Mobile* means to move. Mobile cranes can move from place to place, wherever heavy **loads** need to be lifted.

Boom

Hook

Cab

Outrigger

Mobile cranes might have **caterpillar tracks**, which allow them to move on dirt and gravel. Cranes are quite heavy. Caterpillar tracks help these heavy machines hold the ground better.

This crane runs on wheels. Its boom is folded up.

The outrigger keeps the crane from tipping over as it lifts a heavy load.

Railroad Crane

Railroad cranes run on train tracks. They move loads in and out of train cars. They can lift very heavy loads.

Jib

Bucket

Tracks

These railroad cranes fill train cars with coal and lumber.

Railroad cranes can even lift train cars. Train cars are heavy. In an accident, they may leave the tracks. The cranes can pick them up and put them back on the tracks.

Railroad cranes can only lift things near the tracks.

Telescopic Crane

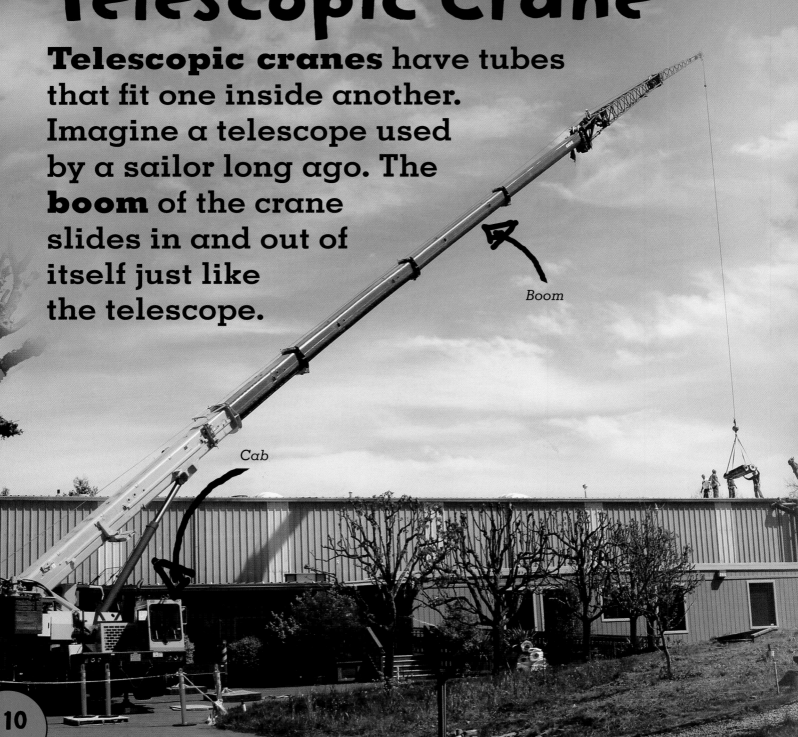

Telescopic cranes have tubes that fit one inside another. Imagine a telescope used by a sailor long ago. The **boom** of the crane slides in and out of itself just like the telescope.

Boom

Cab

This crane has all of the parts of the boom inside the large tube.

Telescopic cranes can reach much farther than regular mobile cranes. They can also become very small. When they are small, they are easy to move from place to place.

A crane operator moves the boom right, left, up, and down to get to the correct position.

11

Tower Crane

A **tower crane** is used to build very tall buildings. The crane may be on the ground or on a floor in the building. As each floor is built, the crane is moved up.

Cab

Mast

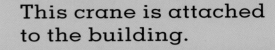

This crane is attached to the building.

Trolley

Working arm

One side of the crane carries the load. The other side holds concrete. This keeps the crane from tipping over. The heavier the load, the more concrete the crane needs.

Construction sites may have many tower cranes.

All-terrain Crane

Some cranes go where there is no road. **All-terrain cranes** have tall wheels that allow them to drive off-road. The cranes can pass over plants without getting stuck in them.

Steel cables

All-terrain tires

Imagine an electric company wanting to put in new lines on a farm. The all-terrain crane could drive in the fields to lift the power poles.

This small all-terrain crane can drive in small spaces.

The tires on all-terrain cranes hold the ground better than regular tires.

Crawler Crane

Crawler cranes drive short distances while carrying loads. They use caterpillar tracks to hold them tightly to the ground. They are extremely heavy, so they usually stay in one area.

Controls

Outrigger

The caterpillar tracks do not move as fast as tires.

Boom

Crawler cranes can lift very heavy loads. A small crawler crane can lift the weight of a humpback whale. Large crawler cranes can lift more than eight times as much!

Look how small the man is compared to the crane.

Bucket

Gantry Crane

A **gantry crane** holds rails, like train tracks, up in the air. Steel cables hold up the rails.

Steel cables

Rail

Upright

The trolley on the gantry crane goes back and forth.

A **hoist** is attached to the trolley. The hoist is a big pulley with a hook on the end. The trolley moves back and forth. The hoist raises and lowers the load.

These gantry cranes load cargo onto ships.

Trolley

Hoist

Overhead Crane

An **overhead crane** is like a gantry crane. The rails on an overhead crane are between the uprights.

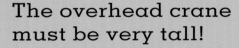

The overhead crane must be very tall!

Trolley

Hoist

Uprights

Overhead cranes may be part of a factory's ceiling. They can lift a whole small boat or build a big ship by lifting its different parts.

This overhead crane is strong enough to lift a boat.

Floating Crane

A **floating crane** does what the name says. It floats. It has no wheels or tracks. Some floating cranes are part of boats. Some floating cranes are an entire boat.

These huge cranes do not sink in the water!

Rotors

Cab

Buckets

Floating cranes can help build bridges. They can pull up sunken ships. Floating cranes can also work on oil rigs in the water.

This crane carries small loads.

Aerial Crane

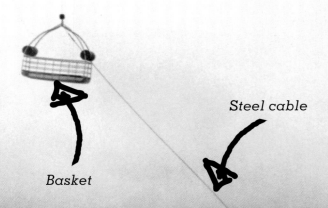

Cockpit

Steel cable

Basket

The word *aerial* means *in the air*. An **aerial crane** hangs from a helicopter. It can lift heavy loads that other cranes can't reach. It is also called a skycrane.

This aerial crane sends a basket to the boat. The basket can carry supplies, people, or both!

**Aerial cranes
are very strong.**

Imagine a tall building that has a large, old air conditioner on the roof. An aerial crane can take it off the roof and set it on the ground. An aerial crane can even lift cars.

Cranes move on wheels, rails, and caterpillar tracks. Some cranes work on the water, and others hang from helicopters. Cranes are even part of factory buildings.

Telescopic Crane

Overhead Crane

Cranes are important machines. They help builders, railroads, and shipping companies. They lift, lower, and move heavy loads that people could not do alone.

All-terrain Crane

Railroad Crane

Amazing Facts

- Operators must pass a test in order to work a crane.

- The largest gantry crane was built and used in Sweden. In 2002 a South Korean company bought it. The crane had to be taken apart, shipped to South Korea, and then rebuilt.

- In 2004 a telescopic crane lifted celebrity Daisy Fuentes 45 feet into the air in New York City to finish creating a billboard.

- "Yoshida" is Japan's largest floating crane. It is as tall as the Great Pyramid of Giza in Egypt!

- The most well-known aerial crane fights fires in Australia. The company that made it named it "Elvis."

- In the 1950s, a crane sunk completely in the sand when building a lake in Nebraska. It is still at the bottom of the lake today.

Glossary

aerial crane a crane that hangs from a helicopter

all-terrain crane a crane that can travel off-road

boom a long beam that helps move loads on a crane

caterpillar tracks tracks with ridges that can hold machines more tightly to the ground than wheels can

crane a machine that lifts, lowers, and moves loads

crawler crane a crane with caterpillar tracks; it moves heavy loads short distances

floating crane an overhead crane with rails held by steel cables

gantry crane an overhead crane with uprights and rails held by steel cables

load the things that a truck, wagon, or person carries

mobile crane a crane that can be moved from place to place

overhead crane a crane that hangs from tracks above it

railroad crane a crane that travels on railroad tracks

telescopic crane a crane with a boom made of tubes that can expand and contract

tower crane a crane used to build a tall building; it has a load on one side of the boom and cement on the other to balance it

Index

Web Finder

http://science.howstuffworks.com/tower-crane.htm

http://science.howstuffworks.com/hydraulic-crane.htm

http://www.heavyequipment.com/crane.php